Life Cycle of a

Butterfly

Angela Royston

Heinemann
LIBRARY

First published in Great Britain by Heinemann Library
Halley Court, Jordan Hill, Oxford OX2 8EJ,
a division of Reed Educational and Professional Publishing Ltd.

Heinemann is a registered trademark of Reed Educational and Professional
Publishing Limited.

Oxford   Melbourne   Auckland   Kuala Lumpur   Singapore
Ibadan   Nairobi   Kampala   Johannesburg   Gaborone
Portsmouth NH (USA)   Chicago

Designed by Celia Floyd
Illustrations by Alan Fraser
Printed in Hong Kong / China

03 02 01 00 99
10 9 8 7 6 5 4 3 2 1

ISBN 0 431 08375 4
This title is also available in a hardback edition (ISBN 0 431 08366 5)

British Library Cataloguing in Publication Data

Royston, Angela
Life cycle of a butterfly
1. Butterflies – Juvenile literature
I. Title II. Butterfly
595.7'89

Acknowledgements
The Publisher would like to thank the following for permission to reproduce
photographs:
A–Z Botanical Collection Ltd/N K D Miller pg 4; Bruce Coleman Ltd/Frans Lanting
pgs 26-27, Bruce Coleman Ltd/Andrew J Purcell pg 18, Bruce Coleman Ltd/John Shaw
pg 11; Dembinsky Photo Association/S Moody pg 10; NHPA/Dr Eckart Pott pgs 21,
22, NHPA/John Shaw pg 5, NHPA/Rod Planck pg 12; Oxford Scientific Films/Breck P
Kent pgs 6, 8, Oxford Scientific Films/JAL Cooke pgs 7, 24, 25, Oxford Scientific
Films/Rudie H Kuiter pgs 9, 14, 15, 16, 17, Oxford Scientific Films/Tom Ulrich pg 12,
Oxford Scientific Films/Harry Fox pg 19, Oxford Scientific Films/Norbert Wu pg 20,
Oxford Scientific Films/Dan Guravich pg 23.

Cover photograph: Superstock.

Our thanks to Anthony M V Hoare, Butterfly Conservation, for his comments in the
preparation of this edition.

Contents

	page
What is a butterfly?	4
Butterfly eggs	6
A few days later	8
1 week	10
2 weeks	12
4 weeks	14
6 weeks	16
8 weeks	18
10 weeks	20
14–30 weeks	22
32 weeks	24
The journey continues	26
Life cycle	28
Fact file	30
Glossary	31
Index	32

What is a butterfly?

A butterfly is an insect. It has six legs, four wings and two **antennae**. Many butterflies have brightly coloured wings, like this swallowtail.

 1 day 1 week 4 weeks 6 weeks

Many kinds of butterflies live in different parts of the world. The butterfly in this book is a Monarch butterfly from North America.

10 weeks

32 weeks

33 weeks

Butterfly eggs

Every butterfly begins life as a tiny egg. The Monarch butterfly lays her eggs on a **milkweed** leaf. Just over a week later, the egg begins to **hatch**.

I day I week 4 weeks 6 weeks

A small **caterpillar** crawls out of
the egg! It ate a hole in the egg
and now it will eat the eggshell.

A few days later

The **caterpillar** eats and grows
bigger. It chews through the leaf with
its strong **jaws**. Soon it has eaten a
big hole in the **milkweed** leaf.

1 day

1 week

4 weeks

6 weeks

All the eggs have **hatched** and many Monarch caterpillars are feeding on the milkweed plant. They crawl from leaf to leaf, eating as they go.

10 weeks

32 weeks

33 weeks

I week

The **caterpillar** is growing, but its skin is not. One day its skin is so tight it splits open. The caterpillar has a new and bigger skin underneath!

I day

I week

4 weeks

6 weeks

The caterpillar will shed its skin four times as it grows. Now it crawls away, clinging to the thin stem with its many legs.

2 weeks

The **caterpillar** eats and grows. It is not eaten by other animals, because **milkweed** leaves contain something that makes the caterpillar taste nasty.

1 day   1 week   4 weeks   6 weeks

This bird catches insects, but when it sees the Monarch caterpillar's black and yellow stripes, it leaves it alone. The bird has learned that the Monarch tastes nasty.

10 weeks

32 weeks

33 weeks

4 weeks

When the **caterpillar** is fully grown it **spins** a silky pad on a leaf. It grasps the pad and its stripy skin splits for the last time.

1 day

1 week

4 weeks

6 weeks

Underneath the skin is a green **pupa**. The caterpillar is ready to change into a butterfly!

10 weeks

32 weeks

33 weeks

6 weeks

Inside the hard shell of the **pupa**, the **caterpillar's** body changes. Then the pupa cracks open and the butterfly pulls itself free.

1 day

1 week

4 weeks

6 weeks

At first its wings
are damp and
crumpled, but,
as they dry, the
wings slowly
open. Now the
butterfly is ready
to fly away.

10 weeks

32 weeks

33 weeks

8 weeks

The butterfly flits from flower to flower, feeding on their **nectar**. It uncoils its long tongue and sucks up the sweet juice.

1 day

1 week

4 weeks

6 weeks

Birds do not try to catch it. The chemicals that made the **caterpillar** taste nasty are still in its body, making it taste nasty too.

10 weeks

32 weeks

33 weeks

10 weeks

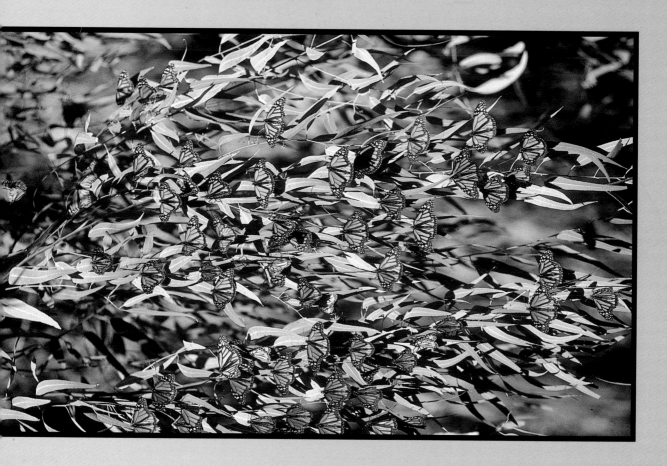

It is autumn and the weather is getting very cold. The Monarch butterflies gather together on the branches of trees.

I day

I week

4 weeks

6 weeks

Suddenly they all flutter up into the sky. They fly south until they reach the mountains of Mexico, where the weather is warmer even in winter.

10 weeks

32 weeks

33 weeks

14–30 weeks

The butterflies are very tired. They gather on a pine tree to rest and sleep for the winter.

I day   I week   4 weeks 6 weeks

When spring comes, the sun warms
the butterflies and wakes them up.
They feed from the flowers and most
of the butterflies start to fly north.

10 weeks

32 weeks

33 weeks

32 weeks

The butterflies rest during the journey. This male has found a female that is ready to **mate**. After mating, the female lays her eggs.

1 day

1 week

4 weeks

6 weeks

She lays them on a **milkweed** plant. The butterflies live only for a few more weeks, but, by then, new **caterpillars** are **hatching**.

10 weeks

32 weeks

33 weeks

The journey continues

Back in Mexico, these butterflies have been battered by a big storm. Some recover and will fly north. Others will die on the journey.

I day I week 4 weeks 6 weeks

But along the way, **caterpillars** are **hatching**. When they change into butterflies they too will fly north. There they will **mate** and lay eggs of their own.

10 weeks

32 weeks

33 weeks

Life cycle

Egg hatching

1 week

4 weeks

6 weeks

10 weeks

32 weeks

33 weeks

Fact file

The wingspan of a Monarch butterfly is about 10 centimetres, nearly as wide as your hand span.

Monarchs fly further than any other kind of butterfly. During their long journeys north and south they fly up to 3000 kilometres.

Butterflies use their **antennae** to smell and to feel. They smell food and the special chemicals a male Monarch gives off when he is trying to **mate**.

In one day, a **caterpillar** may eat many times its own weight in leaves.

Glossary

antennae the feelers on an insect's head

caterpillar a young butterfly or moth before it changes into a **pupa**

hatch to break out of an egg

jaws the moving parts of the **caterpillar's** mouth

mate to come together (a male and a female) to produce young

milkweed a kind of plant

nectar the sweet juice produced by some flowers

pupa the stage in life when a **caterpillar** changes into a butterfly or moth

spin to make a long thread

Index

antennae 4, 30, 31

bird 13, 19

butterfly 15–18, 20, 22–27, 30, 31

caterpillar 7, 8–16, 19, 25, 27, 30, 31

egg 6, 7, 9, 24, 25, 27, 31

flower 18, 23

jaws 8, 31

milkweed leaf 6, 8, 9, 12, 25, 31

nectar 18, 31

pupa 15, 16, 31

skin 10, 11, 14

stem 11, 31

wings 4, 17, 30